EAGLE® BRAND

Cookies & Treats

Creamy Baked Cheesecake	4
Raspberry Topping	4
Magic Cookie Bars	6
Key Lime Pie	8
Lemon Crumb Bars	10
White Chocolate Squares	12
Chocolate Chiffon Pie	14
Fudge Ribbon Sheet Cake	16
Cookies 'n' Crème Fudge	18
No-Bake Peanutty Chocolate Drops	18
Candy Bar Bars	20
Double Chocolate Brownies	21
Triple Chocolate Cheesecakes	22
Chocolate Peanut Butter Dessert Sauce	24
Coconut Macaroons	24
Chocolate Almond Torte	26
Chocolate Almond Frosting	26
Raspberry Almond Trifles	28
Chocolate Chip Treasure Cookies	30

Creamy Baked Cheesecake

Prep Time: 25 minutes   **Bake Time:** 55 to 60 minutes

1¼ cups graham cracker crumbs
¼ cup sugar
⅓ cup (⅔ stick) butter or margarine, melted
2 (8-ounce) packages cream cheese, softened
1 (14-ounce) can Eagle® Brand Sweetened Condensed Milk
    (NOT evaporated milk)
3 eggs
¼ cup ReaLemon® Lemon Juice from Concentrate
1 (8-ounce) container sour cream, at room temperature
    Raspberry Topping (recipe follows, optional)

1. Preheat oven to 300°F. Combine crumbs, sugar and butter; press firmly on bottom of ungreased 9-inch springform pan.

2. In large bowl, beat cream cheese until fluffy.

3. Gradually beat in **Eagle Brand** until smooth. Add eggs and **ReaLemon;** mix well. Pour into prepared pan.

4. Bake 50 to 55 minutes or until set.

5. Remove from oven; top with sour cream. Bake 5 minutes longer. Cool. Chill. Prepare Raspberry Topping and serve with cheesecake. Store covered in refrigerator.   *Makes 1 (9-inch) cheesecake*

Raspberry Topping

Prep Time: 5 minutes

1 (10-ounce) package thawed frozen red raspberries in syrup
¼ cup red currant jelly or red raspberry jam
1 tablespoon cornstarch

1. Drain ⅔ cup syrup from raspberries.

2. In small saucepan over medium heat, combine syrup, jelly and cornstarch. Cook and stir until slightly thickened and clear. Cool. Stir in raspberries.

New York Style Cheesecake: Increase cream cheese to 4 (8-ounce) packages and eggs to 4. Proceed as directed, adding 2 tablespoons flour after eggs. Bake 1 hour 10 minutes or until center is set. Omit sour cream. Cool. Chill. Serve and store as directed.

Magic Cookie Bars

Prep Time: 10 minutes   **Bake Time:** 25 minutes

> ½ cup (1 stick) butter or margarine
> 1½ cups graham cracker crumbs
> 1 (14-ounce) can Eagle® Brand Sweetened Condensed Milk
>   (NOT evaporated milk)
> 2 cups (12 ounces) semi-sweet chocolate chips
> 1⅓ cups flaked coconut
> 1 cup chopped nuts

1. Preheat oven to 350°F (325°F for glass dish). In 13×9-inch baking pan, melt butter in oven.

2. Sprinkle crumbs over butter; pour **Eagle Brand** evenly over crumbs. Layer evenly with remaining ingredients; press down firmly.

3. Bake 25 minutes or until lightly browned. Cool. Chill if desired. Cut into bars. Store loosely covered at room temperature.

Makes 24 to 36 bars

7-Layer Magic Cookie Bars: Substitute 1 cup (6 ounces) butterscotch-flavored chips* for 1 cup semi-sweet chocolate chips and proceed as directed above.

*Peanut butter-flavored chips or white chocolate chips may be substituted for butterscotch-flavored chips.

Magic Peanut Cookie Bars: Substitute 2 cups (about ¾ pound) chocolate-covered peanuts for semi-sweet chocolate chips and chopped nuts.

Magic Rainbow Cookie Bars: Substitute 2 cups plain candy-coated chocolate candies for semi-sweet chocolate chips.

Top to bottom: 7-Layer Magic Cookie Bars
and Magic Rainbow Cookie Bars

Key Lime Pie

Prep Time: 25 minutes   Bake Time: 45 minutes

Cool Time: 1 hour   Chill Time: 3 hours

> **3 eggs, separated**
> **1 (14-ounce) can Eagle® Brand Sweetened Condensed Milk**
>   **(NOT evaporated milk)**
> **½ cup ReaLime® Lime Juice from Concentrate**
> **2 to 3 drops green food coloring (optional)**
> **1 (9-inch) unbaked pie crust**
> **½ teaspoon cream of tartar**
> **⅓ cup sugar**

1. Preheat oven to 325°F. In medium bowl, beat egg yolks; gradually beat in **Eagle Brand** and **ReaLime.** Stir in food coloring. Pour into pie crust.

2. Bake 30 minutes. Remove from oven. Increase oven temperature to 350°F.

3. Meanwhile, for meringue, with clean mixer, beat egg whites and cream of tartar to soft peaks. Gradually beat in sugar, 1 tablespoon at a time. Beat 4 minutes or until stiff, glossy peaks form and sugar is dissolved.

4. Immediately spread meringue over hot pie, carefully sealing to edge of crust to prevent meringue from shrinking. Bake 15 minutes. Cool 1 hour. Chill at least 3 hours. Store covered in refrigerator.

Makes 8 servings

Key Lime Pie

Lemon Crumb Bars

Prep Time: 30 minutes   Bake Time: 35 minutes

1 (18¼-ounce) package lemon or yellow cake mix
½ cup (1 stick) butter or margarine, softened
1 egg plus 3 egg yolks
2 cups finely crushed saltine crackers (¼ pound)
1 (14-ounce) can Eagle® Brand Sweetened Condensed Milk
    (NOT evaporated milk)
½ cup ReaLemon® Lemon Juice from Concentrate

1. Preheat oven to 350°F. Grease 15×10×1-inch baking pan. In large bowl, combine cake mix, butter and 1 egg; mix well (mixture will be crumbly). Stir in cracker crumbs. Reserve 2 cups crumb mixture. Press remaining crumb mixture firmly on bottom of prepared pan. Bake 15 minutes.

2. Meanwhile, in medium bowl, combine egg yolks, **Eagle Brand** and **ReaLemon;** mix well. Spread evenly over baked crust.

3. Top with reserved crumb mixture. Bake 20 minutes or until firm. Cool. Cut into bars. Store covered in refrigerator.

Makes 36 to 48 bars

 *Helpful Hint*

Here's a quick and easy way to make cracker or cookie crumbs: Place crackers in a large resealable plastic food storage bag; seal. Roll a rolling pin over the crackers to crush.

Lemon Crumb Bars

White Chocolate Squares

Prep Time: 15 minutes   **Bake Time:** 20 to 25 minutes

  1 (12-ounce) package white chocolate chips, divided
¼ cup (½ stick) butter or margarine
  2 cups all-purpose flour
½ teaspoon baking powder
  1 (14-ounce) can Eagle® Brand Sweetened Condensed Milk
      (NOT evaporated milk)
  1 cup chopped pecans, toasted
  1 large egg
  1 teaspoon vanilla extract
     Powdered sugar

1. Preheat oven to 350°F. Grease 13×9-inch baking pan. In large saucepan over low heat, melt 1 cup chips and butter. Stir in flour and baking powder until blended. Stir in **Eagle Brand,** pecans, egg, vanilla and remaining chips. Spoon mixture into prepared pan.

2. Bake 20 to 25 minutes. Cool. Sprinkle with powdered sugar; cut into squares. Store covered at room temperature.   *Makes 24 bars*

 *Helpful Hint*

Toasted nuts and coconut give foods a pleasant crunchiness and enhance the food's nutty flavor. To toast, spread the chopped nuts or coconut in a single layer in a shallow baking pan. Preheat the oven to 350°F. Bake 5 to 10 minutes or until light golden brown, stirring frequently to prevent burning.

White Chocolate Squares

Chocolate Chiffon Pie

Prep Time: 20 minutes   **Chill Time:** 3 hours

2 (1-ounce) squares unsweetened chocolate, chopped
1 (14-ounce) can Eagle® Brand Sweetened Condensed Milk
(NOT evaporated milk)
1 envelope unflavored gelatin
⅓ cup water
½ teaspoon vanilla extract
1 cup (½ pint) whipping cream, whipped
1 (6-ounce) ready-made chocolate or graham cracker crumb
pie crust
Additional whipped cream

1. In heavy saucepan over low heat, melt chocolate with **Eagle Brand.** Remove from heat.

2. Meanwhile, in small saucepan, sprinkle gelatin over water; let stand 1 minute. Over low heat, stir until gelatin dissolves.

3. Stir gelatin into chocolate mixture. Add vanilla. Cool to room temperature. Fold in whipped cream. Spread into crust.

4. Chill 3 hours or until set. Garnish with additional whipped cream. Store covered in refrigerator.   *Makes 1 pie*

 *Helpful Hint*

For easy pie-making, nothing beats a ready-made pie crust and Eagle Brand! You'll find graham cracker and chocolate-flavored crumb crusts as well as pastry mixes in 1- and 2-crust sizes in the baking aisle of most supermarkets.

Chocolate Chiffon Pie

Fudge Ribbon Sheet Cake

Prep Time: 20 minutes   **Bake Time:** 40 minutes

1 (18¼-ounce) package chocolate cake mix
1 (8-ounce) package cream cheese, softened
2 tablespoons butter or margarine, softened
1 tablespoon cornstarch
1 (14-ounce) can Eagle® Brand Sweetened Condensed Milk
    (NOT evaporated milk)
1 egg
1 teaspoon vanilla extract
  Chocolate Glaze (recipe follows)

1. Preheat oven to 350°F. Grease and flour 13×9-inch baking pan. Prepare cake mix as package directs. Pour batter into prepared pan.

2. In small bowl, beat cream cheese, butter and cornstarch until fluffy. Gradually beat in **Eagle Brand.** Add egg and vanilla; beat until smooth. Spoon evenly over cake batter.

3. Bake 40 minutes or until wooden pick inserted near center comes out clean. Cool. Prepare Chocolate Glaze and drizzle over cake. Store covered in refrigerator.   *Makes 10 to 12 servings*

Chocolate Glaze
In small saucepan over low heat, melt 1 (1-ounce) square unsweetened or semi-sweet chocolate and 1 tablespoon butter or margarine with 2 tablespoons water. Remove from heat. Stir in ¾ cup powdered sugar and ½ teaspoon vanilla extract. Stir until smooth and well blended. Makes about ⅓ cup.

Fudge Ribbon Bundt Cake: Preheat oven to 350°F. Grease and flour 10-inch bundt pan. Prepare cake mix as package directs. Pour batter into prepared pan. Prepare cream cheese topping as directed above; spoon evenly over batter. Bake 50 to 55 minutes or until wooden pick inserted near center comes out clean. Cool 10 minutes. Remove from pan. Cool. Prepare Chocolate Glaze and drizzle over cake. Store covered in refrigerator.

Fudge Ribbon Sheet Cake

Cookies 'n' Crème Fudge

Prep Time: 10 minutes   Chill Time: 2 hours

> **3 (6-ounce) packages white chocolate baking squares**
> **1 (14-ounce) can Eagle® Brand Sweetened Condensed Milk**
>   **(NOT evaporated milk)**
> **⅛ teaspoon salt**
> **2 cups coarsely crushed chocolate crème-filled sandwich**
>   **cookies (about 20 cookies)**

1. Line 8-inch square baking pan with foil. In heavy saucepan over low heat, melt chocolate with **Eagle Brand** and salt. Remove from heat. Stir in crushed cookies. Spread evenly in prepared pan. Chill 2 hours or until firm.

2. Turn fudge onto cutting board. Peel off foil; cut into squares. Store tightly covered at room temperature.

Makes about 2½ pounds

No-Bake Peanutty Chocolate Drops

Prep Time: 10 minutes   Chill Time: 2 hours

> **½ cup (1 stick) butter or margarine**
> **⅓ cup unsweetened cocoa**
> **1 (14-ounce) can Eagle® Brand Sweetened Condensed Milk**
>   **(NOT evaporated milk)**
> **2½ cups quick-cooking oats**
> **1 cup chopped peanuts**
> **½ cup peanut butter**

1. Line baking sheets with waxed paper. In medium saucepan over medium heat, melt butter; stir in cocoa. Bring mixture to a boil.

2. Remove from heat; stir in remaining ingredients.

3. Drop by teaspoonfuls onto prepared baking sheets; chill 2 hours or until set. Store loosely covered in refrigerator.

Makes about 5 dozen

Cookies 'n' Crème Fudge

Candy Bar Bars

Prep Time: 20 minutes   Bake Time: 40 minutes

¾ cup (1½ sticks) butter or margarine, softened
¼ cup peanut butter
1 cup packed brown sugar
1 teaspoon baking soda
2 cups quick-cooking oats
1½ cups all-purpose flour
1 egg
1 (14-ounce) can Eagle® Brand Sweetened Condensed Milk
   (NOT evaporated milk)
4 cups chopped candy bars (such as chocolate-coated
   caramel-topped nougat bars with peanuts,
   chocolate-covered crisp wafers, chocolate-covered
   caramel-topped cookie bars, or chocolate-covered
   peanut butter cups)

1. Preheat oven to 350°F. In large bowl, combine butter and peanut butter. Add sugar and baking soda; beat well. Stir in oats and flour. Reserve 1¾ cups crumb mixture.

2. Stir egg into remaining crumb mixture; press firmly on bottom of ungreased 15×10×1-inch baking pan. Bake 15 minutes.

3. Spread **Eagle Brand** over baked crust. Stir together reserved crumb mixture and candy bar pieces; sprinkle evenly over top. Bake 25 minutes or until golden. Cool. Cut into bars. Store covered at room temperature.

Makes 48 bars

Double Chocolate Brownies

Prep Time: 15 minutes   **Bake Time:** 35 minutes

1¼ cups all-purpose flour, divided
¼ cup sugar
½ cup (1 stick) cold butter or margarine
1 (14-ounce) can Eagle® Brand Sweetened Condensed Milk
   (NOT evaporated milk)
¼ cup unsweetened cocoa
1 egg
1 teaspoon vanilla extract
½ teaspoon baking powder
1 (8-ounce) milk chocolate bar, broken into chunks
¾ cup chopped nuts (optional)

1. Preheat oven to 350°F. Line 13×9-inch baking pan with foil; set aside.

2. In medium bowl, combine 1 cup flour and sugar; cut in butter until crumbly. Press firmly on bottom of prepared pan. Bake 15 minutes.

3. In large bowl, beat **Eagle Brand,** cocoa, egg, remaining ¼ cup flour, vanilla and baking powder. Stir in chocolate chunks and nuts. Spread over baked crust. Bake 20 minutes or until set.

4. Cool. Use foil to lift out of pan. Cut into bars. Store tightly covered at room temperature.   *Makes 24 brownies*

Triple Chocolate Cheesecakes

Prep Time: 20 minutes   **Chill Time:** 4 hours

1 envelope unflavored gelatin
½ cup cold water
1 (14-ounce) can Eagle® Brand Sweetened Condensed Milk
    (NOT evaporated milk)
2 (8-ounce) packages cream cheese, softened
4 (1-ounce) squares unsweetened chocolate, melted and slightly
    cooled
1 (8-ounce) carton frozen non-dairy whipped topping, thawed
½ cup (3 ounces) mini chocolate chips
1 (21-ounce) can cherry pie filling (optional)
2 (6-ounce) ready-made chocolate crumb pie crusts

1. In 1-cup glass measure, stir together gelatin and cold water; let
stand 5 minutes to soften. Pour about 1 inch water into small
saucepan; place glass measure in saucepan. Place saucepan over
medium heat; stir until gelatin is dissolved. Remove measure from
saucepan; cool slightly.

2. In large bowl, combine **Eagle Brand,** cream cheese and melted
chocolate; beat until smooth. Gradually beat in gelatin mixture. Fold
in whipped topping and chips.

3. Spread pie filling on bottoms of crusts, if desired. Spoon
chocolate mixture into pie crusts. Cover and chill at least 4 hours.
Store covered in refrigerator.

Makes 2 cheesecakes (12 servings total)

Tip: To store this cheesecake in the freezer, cover and freeze up to
1 month. Serve frozen, or remove from freezer several hours before
serving and let thaw in the refrigerator.

Triple Chocolate Cheesecake

Chocolate Peanut Butter Dessert Sauce

Prep Time: 15 minutes

   2 (1-ounce) squares semi-sweet chocolate, chopped
   2 tablespoons creamy peanut butter
   1 (14-ounce) can Eagle® Brand Sweetened Condensed Milk
      (NOT evaporated milk)
   2 tablespoons milk
   1 teaspoon vanilla extract

1. In medium saucepan over medium-low heat, melt chocolate and peanut butter with **Eagle Brand** and milk, stirring constantly.

2. Remove from heat; stir in vanilla. Cool slightly. Serve warm over ice cream, cake or as fruit dipping sauce. Store covered in refrigerator.

Makes about 1½ cups

Coconut Macaroons

Prep Time: 10 minutes   **Bake Time:** 15 to 17 minutes

   1 (14-ounce) can Eagle® Brand Sweetened Condensed Milk
      (NOT evaporated milk)
   2 teaspoons vanilla extract
   1 to 1½ teaspoons almond extract
   2 (7-ounce) packages flaked coconut (5⅓ cups)

1. Preheat oven to 325°F. Line baking sheets with foil; grease and flour foil. Set aside.

2. In large bowl, combine **Eagle Brand,** vanilla and almond extract. Stir in coconut. Drop by rounded teaspoons onto prepared sheets; with spoon, slightly flatten each mound.

3. Bake 15 to 17 minutes or until golden. Remove from baking sheets; cool on wire rack. Store loosely covered at room temperature.

Makes about 4 dozen

Chocolate Peanut Butter Dessert Sauce

Chocolate Almond Torte

Prep Time: 30 minutes   Bake Time: 18 to 20 minutes

    4 eggs, separated
    ½ cup (1 stick) butter or margarine, softened
    1 cup sugar
    1 teaspoon vanilla extract
    1 teaspoon almond extract
    1 cup finely chopped toasted almonds
    ¾ cup all-purpose flour
    ½ cup unsweetened cocoa
    ½ teaspoon baking powder
    ½ teaspoon baking soda
    ⅔ cup milk
    Chocolate Almond Frosting (recipe follows)

Line 2 (8- or 9-inch) round cake pans with waxed paper. Preheat oven to 350°F. In small bowl, beat egg whites until soft peaks form; set aside. In large bowl, beat butter and sugar until fluffy. Add egg yolks and extracts; mix well. In medium bowl, combine almonds, flour, cocoa, baking powder and baking soda; add alternately with milk to butter mixture, beating well after each addition. Fold in beaten egg whites. Pour into prepared pans. Bake 18 to 20 minutes or until wooden pick inserted near center comes out clean. Cool 10 minutes; remove from pans. Cool completely.

Prepare Chocolate Almond Frosting. Split each cake layer; fill and frost with frosting. Garnish as desired. Store covered in refrigerator.

Makes 1 (4-layer) cake

Chocolate Almond Frosting

Prep Time: 20 minutes

    2 (1-ounce) squares semi-sweet chocolate, chopped
    1 (14-ounce) can Eagle® Brand Sweetened Condensed Milk
        (NOT evaporated milk)
    1 teaspoon almond extract

1. In heavy saucepan over medium heat, melt chocolate with **Eagle Brand.** Cook and stir until mixture thickens, about 10 minutes.

2. Remove from heat; cool 10 minutes. Stir in almond extract; cool.

Makes about 1½ cups

Chocolate Almond Torte

Raspberry Almond Trifles

Prep Time: 20 minutes   **Chill Time:** 2 hours

> **2 cups whipping cream**
> **¼ cup plus 1 tablespoon raspberry liqueur or orange juice, divided**
> **1 (14-ounce) can Eagle® Brand Original or Fat Free Sweetened Condensed Milk (NOT evaporated milk)**
> **2 (3-ounce) packages ladyfingers, separated**
> **1 cup seedless raspberry jam**
> **½ cup sliced almonds, toasted**

1. In large bowl, beat whipping cream and 1 tablespoon liqueur until stiff peaks form. Fold in **Eagle Brand;** set aside.

2. Layer bottom of 12 (4-ounce) custard cups or ramekins with ladyfingers. Brush with some remaining liqueur. Spread half of jam over ladyfingers. Spread evenly with half of cream mixture; sprinkle with half of almonds. Repeat layers with remaining ladyfingers, liqueur, jam, cream mixture and almonds. Cover and chill 2 hours. Store covered in refrigerator.   *Makes 12 servings*

 *Helpful Hint*

> *To make a simple party more festive, tie ribbons onto stems of glasses, add a fresh bowl of flowers floating in water, and light a few candles at the dinner or dessert table. Enjoy!*

Raspberry Almond Trifles

Chocolate Chip Treasure Cookies

Prep Time: 15 minutes   **Bake Time:** 9 to 10 minutes

1½ cups graham cracker crumbs
½ cup all-purpose flour
2 teaspoons baking powder
1 (14-ounce) can Eagle® Brand Sweetened Condensed Milk
    (NOT evaporated milk)
½ cup (1 stick) butter or margarine, softened
1⅓ cups flaked coconut
1 (12-ounce) package semi-sweet chocolate chips
1 cup chopped walnuts

1. Preheat oven to 375°F. In small bowl, combine crumbs, flour and baking powder.

2. In large bowl, beat **Eagle Brand** and butter until smooth. Add crumb mixture; mix well. Stir in coconut, chips and walnuts.

3. Drop by rounded tablespoons onto ungreased cookie sheets. Bake 9 to 10 minutes or until lightly browned. Store loosely covered at room temperature.   *Makes about 3 dozen*